T0072590

A Cup of Tea and A Slice of Poetry

A Cup of Tea and A Slice of Poetry

Carol Paxton

Illustrations by Chris Rhodes

authorHOUSE®

AuthorHouse™
1663 Liberty Drive
Bloomington, IN 47403
www.authorhouse.com
Phone: 1-800-839-8640

First published by AuthorHouse   01/28/2012

ISBN: 978-1-4678-8307-8 (sc)

Printed in the United States of America

This book is printed on acid-free paper.

Illustrations by Chris Rhodes

Contents

///

Teddy bears picnic

The teddies have found a patch of ground

They look around no one to be found,

Out of their bag they pull out a rug

A plate, bowl and a mug,

They sink onto the rug and have a drink

Giving them time to think,

What games can we play before we eat?

We could try finding sheep,

Or catch butterflies in our nets

Once decided of they set,

Around the field they ran and jumped

Quite often running into each other with a bump,

Soon their tummy's started to rumble

Can we have our picnic now they began to grumble?

Yes we can said mother bear, we've had enough fresh air,

On the rug they all sat and the picnic, they began to share.

The birth of parenthood

A woman and a man create a child
Something so tiny meek and mild,
Looks so helpless needs some help,
Looks so cold needs some warmth.

As the child becomes older, its demands become more,
It needs time and patience, understanding,
But most of all it needs warmth and love,
From its parents it asks so much.

We try to be there for them all the way
Watching them grow and develop each day,
We sometimes fall along the way
But it's them that keep us going in many away.

When we grow old and weak, the role is reversed,
It is them we look to for help and support,
It is they we ask to guide us each day,
We have them strong and loving so we can ask for their help.

As they grow.

Another year gone by, more independent are they,

Nine, eleven and nearly fourteen my children are doing fine,

From when they were babies in arms,

Each year sails by, into young people they are growing,

Yet me another year, oh dear,

Another pound put on, another grey hair found,

However, they make me proud in all they do,

In addition, I know lovely adults they will be.

A job you never finish

Being a mother is a job for life,
Not as simple as being a wife,
You are on call all day every day,
Your on demanded upon in many a way.

As your child grows older the job tougher,
However, you know you would not swap for another,
You have to train and guide this child,
Sometimes all you want to do is run and hide.

When they go to school, your job gets bigger,
They want your help with every word and figure
To make sure their clothes are neat
In addition, their shoes are clean upon their feet.

C.D. RHODES 06

My Mother said!

Have you washed your face and cleaned your teeth?

Have you brushed your hair and changed your underwear?

Have you put away your toys before you go out with the boys?

Have you made your bed? Are your animals fed?

"I want you back at 5 o'clock as tea will be ready on the dot"!

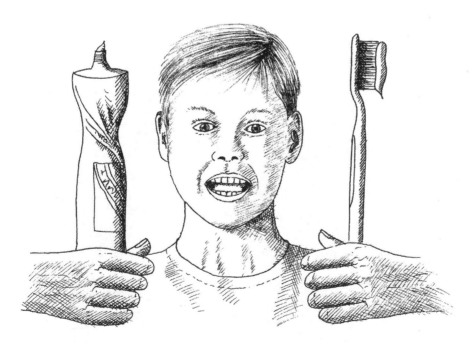

Oh Mothers cleaning!

Do not sit there
I've plumped up the that chair,
Do not touch the screen
It has been cleaned,
Do not come past the door
I have just washed the floor,
Do not touch that dress
It has been through the press,
"What can we do today?"
"PLEASE GO OUT TO PLAY"
I am doing the cleaning,
          OK.

Three lovely kids.

I have three lovely children,
They make you angry,
They make you cross,
However, without them, I would be a total loss.

They're growing fast,
They're going up the school ladder,
Babies they're not any more,
However, young children maturing in their own way.

When you need a cuddle or a love,
They're willing to offer you one,
They love you really, and show this in their own way,
However, like to wind you up as well.

C. D. RHODES 06

Mum

What Mum's do best,

To wipe away a tear and mend the hurt,

Brush knots from our matted hair,

Iron our crumpled clothes,

Polishes our shoes nice and clean,

Helps with homework when we struggle,

Cooks our meals including greens,

In their hearts, they hold us near,

In addition, we know she will always be there.

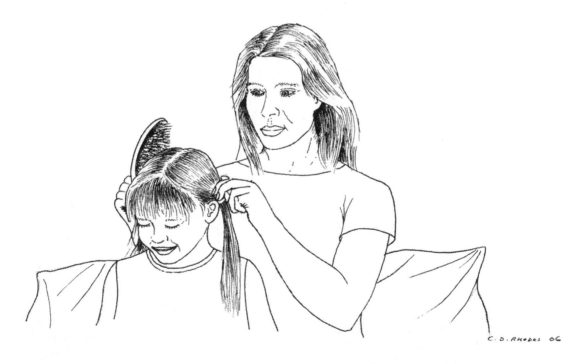

I have a little boy

I have a little boy,

I call him Dan for short,

At Cotswold school, he is taught.

He has a wicked smile,

Deep dark eyes full of mischief,

He can talk mile for mile,

My little boy is he,

He has a heart of gold,

Always loves a cuddle,

His kindness shines so bold,

Always getting in a muddle,

He is my Daniel!

My son's wish

As I put my son to bed,

A wish he made as he laid down his head,

I wish you and Daddy could be together,

Sorry I said it wouldn't be.

His eyes looked at me so sad,

I held him in my arms tight,

It made me feel so bad,

To stay as friends I said we would try to do,

I told him he could always talk to me,

Not to hold it back inside,

His questions I would answer as honestly as I could,

In addition, not make promises that cannot be kept,

I know his pain will take a while to heal,

All I want is for him to be happy,

To not be able to grant his wish hurts inside,

And hopefully in time,

He will trust and confide.

Winter once more

As I walk outside the cold grips my naked hands,
The wind stings my puffed cheeks,
Leaves and twigs crackle under my feet,
It is winter once more.

From brick built chimneys out billows smoke,
Pheasants scurry across the country lanes,
Birds emigrate in hoards through the sky.
It is winter once more.

On my return, the smell of stew meets my cold nose,
The fires roaring to warm my bitter cold hands,
A nice mug of cocoa thaws me out.
It is winter once more.

C. D. RHODES 06

The Hawk and I

Teach me how to protect my own,

Even from when the nest they have flown,

Grip me with your piercing claw,

Show me how to understand pain,

What is life waiting for?

Let me nest with you up high,

Warm and free from the world,

Take me under your widespread wing,

In addition, give me strength to fight each day.

Spike

At the door stood a pile of distressed needles,

No ball of secured round did he make,

He did not retreat across the path,

Wheezing and squeaking he needed help.

We took him in our warm abode,

A bed of cardboard and paper we made,

Dishes of scrumptious food,

Water and milk so weak,

Left he settled for the night.

In the morning he had escaped

We could hear him wheeze as for we could not see him,

Found amongst the washing keeping warm,

Prickles still abstract on his back.

We called the RSPCA they would collect him that day,

They called back said it would be late if they were to call,

For another night he stayed and spike he was named,

A part of the family he had become.

They collected him next day poor chap was in a poor way,
Each week we phoned to see how spike was,
Four weeks we kept up this
He was on the mend putting on weight.
We could collect him, bring him home and let him go,
Back into the bramble bush and winter leaves,
We have not seen him since, he has not been forgotten,
and one day we hope he will return.

A life saved and a friend made,
Creatures of the wild become like a adopted child,
You cannot leave them weak and alone,
They deserve a chance and spike pulled through.

What am I

As darkness falls, I seek light,

As doors open,

Sneak in and hum vigorously round the freshly lit bulb,

Sometimes you may find me where you do not want me,

In your wardrobe keeping warm amongst your clothes.

You will not hear me, and will not be pleased when you find ME!

Along the trust way

As you walk through the door,

Before your eyes, a carpet of colour meets your way,

Reds, oranges, yellow and greens,

Squirrels scuttle up the near naked trees,

While the trees branches dance in the wind.

Crisp under the foot are delicate twigs,

Rainbows of colour flutter through the air,

The air full of the birds songs,

In addition, fields are full of bleating sheep,

As you walk along the way a bench a pleasant treat,

To sit and take in the smells and sounds of the country,

A cocoon of nature new and old,

Each day is different as life forms around us change,

As I walk through the trust door.

Christmas

Christ is born in Bethlehem.

Holly blossoms on the trees green.

Roasted turkey upon your plate.

Invitations to the family to write.

Stockings filled at the end of your bed.

Trees laden with glittering decorations.

Mince pies fresh from the oven.

A child with a gleaming smile.

Sharing a time of giving and receiving.

The life of a tree

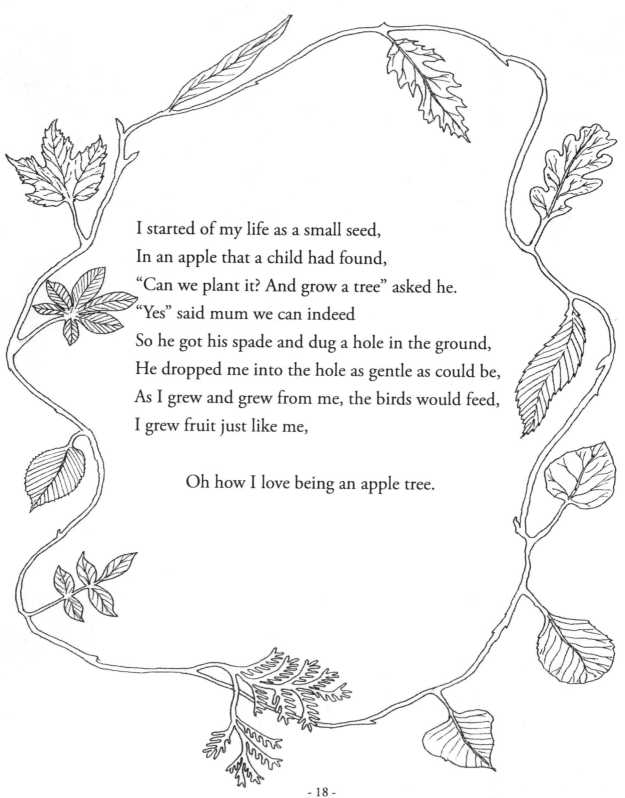

I started of my life as a small seed,
In an apple that a child had found,
"Can we plant it? And grow a tree" asked he.
"Yes" said mum we can indeed
So he got his spade and dug a hole in the ground,
He dropped me into the hole as gentle as could be,
As I grew and grew from me, the birds would feed,
I grew fruit just like me,

Oh how I love being an apple tree.

C. D. Rhodes 06

Winters here

Wellingtons sit ready by the door.

Icicles hang from rooftops.

Nests empty, the young have left.

Trees stand cold and naked.

Evergreens full of lush red berries.

Roaring fires smoking out of chimneys.

Sniffs and snuffles ripe.

Hats and scarves at the ready

Early now evening draws in.

Roads muddy and wet.

Everyone knows winters here.

Stormy weather

The sky is black and heavy,

Thunder like Morse code breaks in and out,

Animals huddled under shaken trees,

Waiting till its over to go back out.

As the rain hits the warm ground,

A vapour of relief releases itself,

The sun breaks through with a glare,

Colourful rays of a rainbow show itself.

Now the damage of the storm can be seen,

Broken branches lay homeless on the ground,

Dry gardens are now slushy wet,

Plenty of food for animals lay across the ground,

The storm has gone.

Conker season

It stands tall and regimented,

Trunk bellowed and green with moss,

Amongst the woodlands, it grows proud,

In autumn off loads its heavy leaves,

The conkers strewn across the woodland floor,

Along come the children with their bags to fill,

Yes, it is conker season once more,

The tree now stands naked and cold,

Waiting for spring, to regroup its spring coat.

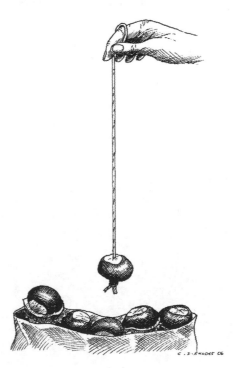

Who am I

I stand tall and uniformed against the hemline of the sky,

My colours dazzle you as you go by,

When the wind does blow, we dance to and fro,

Summer gone once more,

We throw our leaves to the floor.

We cover the ground with a blanket of colour,

Hiding nearly every flower.

We are cold we are bare,

Now what do you see as you stand and stare?

Naked trunks with naked limbs,

Nothing to dazzle you as you go by.

The blanket of snow

As the air warmed,
Snow on the way we were warned,
From the sky white flakes you formed,
On our land, you adorned.
When we look across the vales
Patchwork blankets of snow prevails
Thicker you settle with the gales
Squares of white and green covering the dales,
Birds peck into the gentle snow
Robin's wagtails and a crow,
In the sunlight sparkles show,
Did they find the bread I did throw?
Children out in sledges play
Building snowmen to display,
Sliding down hills all the way,
Watch out more snows coming our way.

Winter

The nights turn in early,
Outside play cut short,
All the trees stand cold and naked,
Little birds fight for food.

Out come hats and gloves,
Winter coats out of storage,
Wellingtons used more now, lots of coughs and colds.

In the skylight burn out their fumes,
Hot water bottles at the ready,
Layers added to shivering bodies,
Everyone is in early now,
Because winters now upon us.

Santa

The children are tucked in bed,
Santa's mince pie and milk wait,
We wait until they're fast asleep,
Oh no forgot the carrot for Rudolph,

Gather stockings laden with goods,
A glass of wine much deserved,
Check to see their sleeping heads,
Lay their stocking by the bed,

Awoken early Morning with gleeful cries,
Santa's been look what we got,
Ok children, please five minute's more,
Nip down put the turkey in,

We give in at six o'clock,
Still tired we've had our lot,
Downstairs bleary eyed,
Look around the Christmas tree,

Shrills of laughter, cries of delight,
He got my letter they chorus together,
Mum open this, mum do this,
Tiredness turns to bliss,
It is nice to see their smiling faces.

Santa has been they have undone the lot.
Presents left in crumpled piles,
Can we go outside to play?
It is another Christmas day.

I can hear, they cannot see.

Did they know I was there?

Quietly sitting on the stairs,

I could see and hear them clear,

They did not know I was sat on the stair.

Yes, they were at it again,

Where did my feelings fit in?

My insides filled with fears,

As my mum was in the kitchen in tears,

Why couldn't they make it work?

Was dad a bad bloke?

Whom would I go with if they split up?

My insides felt sick to the gut,

What I heard, I kept inside.

I did not want to be on the other side,

All I wanted was a family together,

Surely, we could get through this together.

Mum please don't cry

Mum, why are you crying?

I know you do your best and are always trying.

To see you cry hurts me a lot

You think it is your fault when it is not.

Being a mum is not an easy task

Your list of jobs is vast.

However, you are always there for us

When we hurt your there to make a fuss.

If things don't turn out right

You are always there to hold us tight.

So when I see my mum stand and weep

Comfort from us she should seek.

I can't sleep!!!

At last bedtime has arrived I need some sleep.

I will just read a bit of my book then put out the light.

Room now darkness a calm air fills the room.

Oh, I wish I could go to sleep.

It is like this night after night.

Now darkness is outside all I can see is the moon.

I am fed up counting sheep in my head I hear them bleat

Watching the hours rounding the clock what a sight!

I will have to get out of my warm cocoon.

Go downstairs give the kitchen a sweep.

Polish every surface in sight.

I should sleep now I have done every room.

Back I go again to bed straighten out the sheet

Maybe I will fall asleep soon!.

No! I cannot sleep

The card that never arrives

Today is my birthday,

Happy I should be,

But there is something missing,

Which would mean a lot to me?

But there is something missing,

A big or little piece of paper,

The size does not matter at all,

However, every year I keep wishing.

The postman's been I scour the mat,

All I find are bills and brown letters,

But there is something missing,

Who am I kidding there's no chance of that.

Another year without a card,

I feel so deflated and alone,

Have my parents forgot?

Deep down I know there will be no card.

Farewell Sherborne

I am finishing Sherborne School with Robin Hood,

When I started, it was Mrs Wood.

What have I learnt since I have been here?

Things get harder year by year.

To work together and be good friends

To share with each other and learn to lend.

How to learn and enjoy sport

By Mr Mortimore we are taught.

I tried violin and guitar

Then in recorder I got my sliver star

I have learnt to grow and mature

With the teachers help that is for sure.

Many memories I will take with me

As we were like one big family.

(Connor 11)

I remember

I remember,

My first day at School,

I had a nervous tingly feeling in my stomach.

I remember,

The first time I fell over in the playground,

Mrs Hadley helped me.

I remember,

My new friends who played with me in my first playtime,

They are still my friends.

I remember,

The journey to the juniors,

I was excited and nervous,

But soon I settled in.

I remember,

The residential trip to Viney Hill,

My first time away from home,

The climbing low ropes course was such fun,

I didn't want to come home!

I'll remember you all,
And everything I did,
I'll remember you all,
For as long as I live.

(Daniel, aged 11)

Christmas alone

Christmas is a lonely time for most,

Not all the wishes they have come true,

They feel cold and lonely,

Thinking about being on their own,

Their loved ones have left them

Things are not as they used to be,

They do not bother dressing a tree.

They sit and watch through the window,

As people, gaily saunter by,

Yet inside all they do is cry,

The meaning of Christmas is not the same,

There are no presents ready wrapped,

To them Christmas is scrapped,

Why? They have lost their soul mate their best friend,

Christmas used to be for two and now its only one,

Only the memories they once shared with someone they cared,

As today is just another day,

To the rest of us it's Christmas day.

When I grow old

Do not put me in a home
I would be at my house and be alone
I will do my best not to moan
Do not put me in a home.

I want to grow old with grace,
And see the wrinkles grow on my face,
I will still need my own space,
I want to grow old with grace.

If my legs will not work right,
I will use a frame with all my might,
Before I go to bed, I will switch out the light,
If my legs will not work right.

Forty oh no!

//

I looked in the mirror,
Oh no! not me not forty,
I got brave and got nearer,
Yes it's me I am forty.

What have I done in forty years,
School, college,
Work, children, cleaning,
Cooking, washing, charity work.

But I am still forty!

Hedgehog

A little hedgehog hibernating for winter,
Snuggly in a ball he is curled,
Sleeping tightly in his bed of leaves,
We won't see him now till spring begins.

Waking up from his winter sleep,
His spikes are shining and clean,
With his sparking black eyes,
With his long cute ears,
When people come along, Home he runs.

When he shuffles along,
The leaves crunch and crackle,
There glows his black nose,
In spring his new spikes grow,
There he walks along with his pink toes.

Courtney age 6

My soul mate

At last, my soul mate I have found,

A relationship I feel on mutual ground,

He is older than me, wiser then I think,

Always there to pick me up when I feel myself begin to sink,

A traditional country kind of chap,

Always wearing his checked cap,

To tinker in his garage he is content,

Many hours on his tractors, he has spent,

Not one but two little fergies are his passion,

He doesn't care they are old fashioned,

He knows all about them and that is a fact,

His knowledge of the countryside,

Is something to be desired?

With today's kind of farming, he does not agree.

At last, my soul mate I have found,

A relationship I feel on mutual ground.

My confirmation

From our lord I had lost my way,

Feeling troubled and alone,

I thought maybe if I to pray twice a day,

God would know I was trying back to him to roam,

Confirmation was suggested to me,

Was this the road I needed to follow?

Thought about it long and hard hoped it helps me see,

My head full of thoughts my insides still hollow,

Then I felt the time was right for me,

We got to the church emotions running high,

Yes I am here lord I want you by my side,

There were three others my son and I,

As we stood before the bishop, Rev'd Ackerman at our side,

We took our first communion as one,

The church was full of family and friends,

Then I knew my journey had begun.

Joyful warmth around the church descends,

Now we were confirmed and feeling complete,

This time my faith is for keeps.

Amen

Just married

Today has completed my life,
As we are now man and wife,
Together we look ahead
Our hearts with love will, be fed,
For each other we are always there,
In addition, just to tell you how much I care,
And in a 100 years time,
We will remember this as a special time.

C.D.RHODES 06

This book is a combination of poems and sketches married together to give a two sided story to each poem, a written side and a visual side.

The slices of cake represent different poets as displayed in the book. There are poems written by my children and myself. There is nothing more relaxing than sitting down with a cup of tea and digesting some poetry at the same time. The wonderful pen and ink sketches reflect each poem. We hope you enjoy reading and looking at this book, as much as we have had writing and drawing it for you. don't forget your tea!.

Printed in the United States
By Bookmasters